AIR RAID!

JEAN MAY

Illustrated by Kenny McKendry

OXFORD
UNIVERSITY PRESS

OXFORD
UNIVERSITY PRESS

Great Clarendon Street, Oxford OX2 6DP

Oxford University Press is a department of the University of Oxford.
It furthers the University's objective of excellence in research, scholarship,
and education by publishing worldwide in

Oxford   New York

Auckland   Cape Town   Dar es Salaam   Hong Kong   Karachi
Kuala Lumpur   Madrid   Melbourne   Mexico City   Nairobi
New Delhi   Shanghai   Taipei   Toronto

With offices in

Argentina   Austria   Brazil   Chile   Czech Republic   France   Greece
Guatemala   Hungary   Italy   Japan   Poland   Portugal   Singapore
South Korea   Switzerland   Thailand   Turkey   Ukraine   Vietnam

Oxford is a registered trade mark of Oxford University Press
in the UK and in certain other countries

British Library Cataloguing in Publication Data
Data available

ISBN: 978-0-19-918420-0

3 5 7 9 10 8 6 4

Available in packs
Stage 14 More Stories A Pack of 6:
ISBN: 978-0-19-918416-3
Stage 14 More Stories A Class Pack:
ISBN: 978-0-19-918423-1
Guided Reading Cards also available:
ISBN: 978-0-19-918425-5

Cover artwork by Kenny McKendry
Photograph of Jean May by Joseph May

Printed in China by Imago

CHAPTER 1

The bomb

Jack and Harry stared at the bomb for a long time.

'It's bigger than the one that fell on Crown Street,' said Harry.

'Twice as big!' said Jack.

The boys were lying on top of an old warehouse, and by peering over the edge, they could see the bomb clearly.

It had landed in a large crater, but it hadn't exploded, and its nose was buried in the soft earth.

'Wow!' said Harry. 'Wish we could get closer and have a good look. Would you like to touch it, Jack?'

'Touch it!' cried Jack. 'You must be crazy.'

He didn't want to tell his brother, but he was dead scared just looking at it. 'Hey look! There's Old Tin Hat. Watch out. He'll see us.'

Old Tin Hat, the air raid warden, was on duty. It was his job to keep people out of the way until the bomb disposal team arrived. He had roped off the site, and no one could get anywhere near the bomb.

He always chased the boys off. 'You'll get killed, one day!' he'd yell.

But the boys took no notice. Exploring bomb sites was an exciting game, and escaping from Old Tin Hat made it even better.

'Do you think he's scared?' asked Jack.

'No, not Old Tin Hat. He's got no feelings,' said Harry. 'Keep your head down, Jack, we don't want him to see us. You know what he's like – he'll start yelling.'

Old Tin Hat moved away to check some ropes, and the boys pulled themselves to the edge. They had another look at the bomb.

'Why doesn't the bomb disposal come?' asked Jack.

'Too busy,' said Harry. 'They won't defuse this until the morning. Not much to blow up here anyway – most of it's already gone.'

Harry was right. As the brothers gazed round them, they saw heaps of rubble and big holes everywhere. Bits of walls were standing, many of them scorched black by fire. Here and there, scraps of once lovely curtains hung limp and sad.

Harry pointed towards the river. Some seagulls were having a party on an ancient piano which had landed down near the water. A chair was perched crazily on someone's chimney. Earth and brick dust covered everything.

Suddenly Jack felt cold.

'Aw! Come on, Harry. Let's go.'

As the boys scrambled down to the street below, Old Tin Hat spotted them.

'Hoi, you boys!' he shouted.

He waved his arms at a notice –

DANGER
UNEXPLODED
BOMB

'We know! We know!' yelled Harry.

'Well, go on home then,' bawled Old Tin Hat, running towards them with his gas mask bumping around. 'I'll have to see your mother about you again. Now clear off!'

The boys knew that it wasn't a good idea to let Old Tin Hat get too close. They dodged away behind a pile of sandbags.

'Down!' hissed Harry.

They both crouched down out of sight until they heard Old Tin Hat hurrying past. The boys grinned at one another, and then Harry stood up and peered out.

'OK,' he said. 'He's gone.'

'I know!' said Jack. 'Let's go home by Crown Street and see what's left. Mum said it got it bad the other night.'

Harry agreed, and they set off. As they came round the corner, by the bakers at the top of Crown Street, they both gasped with horror.

CHAPTER 2

He's alive!

Crown Street was gone. Most of the houses had been flattened altogether.

Those left standing were badly damaged. Boards covered missing windows and doors, and broken furniture was stacked on the pavement. Crazy heaps of brick and plaster stood where houses had once been.

The boys wandered along in amazement.

Household things lay everywhere. Harry picked up an old umbrella.

There was a broken cup, a wooden spoon, someone's old tin bowl, and a scorched photo of a baby – all scattered about.

'Look at this,' said Harry as he picked up the photo. 'Isn't everything sad here?'

'Yes,' agreed Jack, bleakly.

There was a battered tea caddy lying on the pavement, and he began kicking it along to try and cheer himself up.

Suddenly, Harry grabbed his arm. 'What's that?' he said sharply.

'What's what?'

'Listen.'

There was silence.

'Aw, come on, Harry, it's getting dark. Mum'll be worried.'

'Quiet!' said Harry. 'There it is again.'

A muffled moan came from somewhere nearby, and as the boys listened there came another moan, followed by a faint scratching noise.

'It's over there,' shouted Harry, pointing to a pile of rubble, 'where number ten used to be. It's odd,' he continued, as they hurried towards the sound, 'because the old lady in this house got killed. I heard Mum telling Grandad. Everyone thought it was shocking.'

They both scrambled about in the rubble.

'She did have a dog,' said Jack, suddenly. 'I bet that's it! I bet everyone thought that the dog was dead as well!'

'You're right – she did have a dog – a big shaggy one,' said Harry, excitedly. 'Here boy! Good dog! Good dog!'

An answering whine seemed to come from under the ground, followed by frantic scratching.

'Must be in the old cellar,' cried Harry. 'Quick! Let's clear away all this mess.'

As they started to pull away some planks of splintered wood, there came a muffled growl.

'He's under here all right,' said Jack, yanking and pulling for all he was worth.

A heavy door was wedged in the ground. They both heaved at it, gasping and straining until the door came away in a cloud of dust and stones. The boys reeled back, coughing and spluttering.

Then, when the dust had cleared, they peered down the hole.

'Can't see a thing,' said Harry. He shone his pocket torch down inside. 'Yes! There he is! Right at the bottom of the steps. I think he's trapped. The wall must have fallen in on top of him.'

The dog growled softly, and two big brown eyes, full of hope, looked up at the boys.

'Poor dog,' said Jack. 'We've got to get him out, Harry. He must have been down there for three days – ever since the bombs dropped.'

'We'll get him out,' replied Harry. 'Grab hold of my legs.'

He put the torch in his mouth and inched his way down the steps on his hands.

Jack held tight to Harry's legs, trying hard not to fall into the hole himself.

After a lot of puffing and heaving, Harry managed to reach the bottom of the steps where the dog was trapped.

He rested his torch on one of the steps. Then he started laughing.

'Ugh! He's licking my face all over.'

'Is there a name on his collar?' called Jack.

'I can't see very well. R-A-something,' said Harry.

'Raf! That's it. She had a son in the R.A.F. I remember Mum saying. He's an engineer like Dad. Raf! Raf! Good boy Raf!'

At the sound of his name the dog gave a bark, and he scrambled madly to get free.

'Good boy, Raf. We'll soon have you out of here,' said Harry. 'Whatever you do, don't let go of my legs, Jack.'

Harry began tearing at the rubble around Raf's tail and back. Jack could hear him talking soothingly to the dog as he struggled to set him free.

Suddenly, the mournful notes of the siren began wailing around them. Searchlights lit up and fanned across the sky. Jack was scared.

'It's an air raid, Harry! Hurry up! Come on, hurry up!'

'Shut up!' yelled Harry. 'Just don't let go of my legs.'

He was working very hard. Jack could hear him gasping and grunting at the bottom of the steps.

They both knew that enemy planes had been spotted because the boomp, boomp, boomp, of ack-ack guns started up from way down the river.

Jack pulled hard at Harry's legs. 'They're coming, Harry. The planes are coming!'

'So are we,' shouted Harry, and he and Raf tumbled out of the hole together.

Raf was a big dog, and as he shook himself, clouds of plaster dust flew out of his coat.

All three of them sneezed and coughed. Raf looked sadly at his tail. It was very squashed.

'Brave dog, Raf,' said the boys.

Raf tried a small wag of his tail.
It worked! He wagged it joyfully and
jumped up at Harry, licking him all over.

'He's a smasher,' laughed Harry. 'I'm
glad we found him.'

The boomp, boomp of gunfire was getting louder, and a red glow lit up the night sky.

They could hear the deep droning of enemy aircraft, and knew that the nearby docks were being bombed.

'Come on, Jack. There's nowhere safe round here. We've got to go quick!'

Both boys began racing towards home as fast as they could go, and Raf joined in beside them.

As they were running, they became aware of a new noise. A swishing, whooshing, whistling sound.

'Down!' yelled Harry.

He clutched Raf round the neck and flung himself to the ground. Jack landed beside him.

A booming explosion filled their heads. The world shook. Lumps of brick and earth spattered down around them.

There was the terrifying crump of a building collapsing nearby.

'Jack, Jack – are you OK?' shouted Harry in alarm, clinging on to Raf's collar and reaching out to his brother.

'I'm OK. I'm OK,' said Jack, scrambling to his feet.

They ran on until the breath hurt in their throats. The noise of gun-fire and the terrifying drone of aircraft overhead was joined by the frantic ringing of ambulance and fire-engine bells.

The air became hazy with smoke, and as the boys rounded the top of Crown Street, they saw a row of shops ablaze.

'Look at that!' panted Harry.

The road was full of fire-engines and hoses, and firemen fighting to get their ladders in position. One of them yelled to the boys, 'Not down 'ere, lads! You get 'ome, quick!'

CRUMP! There was a loud bang and they saw an old church on the other side of the road fall in. Its magnificent steeple crumpled instantly, and became another pile of rubble.

'Other way,' gasped Harry, and the boys streaked off, Raf sticking close beside them. They didn't need to use a torch. So many buildings were on fire that it was as bright as day.

Ambulance and fire-engine bells seemed to be ringing everywhere.

Jack's legs ached. 'Mum'll be mad when we get home,' he wheezed.

'If we get home,' gasped Harry. 'Come on! Down here.'

CHAPTER 3

One too many

He rushed through a dark doorway pulling Jack with him, and snapped on his torch.

'Down these steps,' he said, urgently.

Suddenly it was quiet. They could hear Raf's paws clicking down the steps ahead of them.

Jack clattered down behind his brother, finding his own torch now. He was glad to be away from the frightening din in the street.

'Where is this?'

'It's the wine cellars,' said Harry. 'I've never seen that door open before – it must be the blast from the bombs.'

They got to the bottom of the steps and stared round. The whole place was built of stone. Racks and racks of bottles and barrels lined the walls. Huge barrels stood on the floor, and cases of wine were stacked everywhere. It was silent and peaceful.

'We can stay down here until the raid is over,' said Jack, grinning with relief.

Harry smiled. 'It's so quiet down here. You'd never think there was a war on.'

Raf began to sniff about, and the boys followed him, gazing at the bottles.

They were mostly very dusty, and the spiders had had a good time spinning webs from cork to cork.

Suddenly they heard a distant thud from somewhere above in the street. The boys felt the floor shake.

'Sounds like another building gone,' said Harry. 'Hey – look at that barrel! Wow!'

There was a terrible rumbling sound, and a barrel rolled forward off its shelf.

It tumbled on to a rack of bottles. The whole thing sagged as most of the bottles smashed open.

Wine spilled and gurgled on to the stone floor, and soon pools of wine glittered in the torchlight.

Raf jumped forward, wagging his tail. He lapped gratefully at the puddles.

'He *is* thirsty,' laughed Jack. 'Look at him!'

Raf was really enjoying himself. He tasted all the puddles in turn, lapping greedily.

Jack tasted some. 'Ugh!' he said. 'Nasty sour stuff. He must be thirsty to drink that.'

'I bet you'd drink it if you'd been trapped in a dusty cellar for three d...'

Harry stopped speaking and caught his breath.

'Oh, no! Look at the steps!'

Jack stumbled after Harry as he rushed back to the steps. The walls on either side of the entrance had fallen in. The way out was blocked.

'It must have been that crash we heard when the barrel rolled off the shelf,' cried Jack. 'Harry, what shall we do? Nobody knows we're down these cellars. Even if we shouted all night no one would hear us. We'll never get out. We'll end up like those old bottles – all covered in cobwebs!'

'Shut up, Jack! What rubbish. Of course we'll get out,' snapped Harry, trying to sound brave. 'There must be another way out. The wine used to be unloaded and brought in from the river. All we have to do is to find the doors.'

He shone his torch deep into the far end of the cellar.

'Come on, and keep together.'

The place was like a huge underground cavern. They moved along slowly, searching in the torchlight.

Raf padded after them, tasting puddles as he went.

They saw a pair of huge wooden doors
high up in the wall. 'What kind of door
is that?' asked Jack. 'That's no use to
anyone.'

'It's where they used to bring the wine in from the river, before the war,' said Harry with relief. 'Come on! We'll soon be out of here.'

The doors were kept closed with a huge metal rod and Jack had to climb on to Harry's shoulders to reach it. After a struggle, Jack managed to loosen it. The doors creaked open.

The boys scrambled up and through the opening. They found themselves looking down a long dark tunnel.

They could hear water dripping in the distance, and the walls of the tunnel shone wetly in the beams of torchlight.

Raf had a bit of trouble climbing up, and Harry had to yank him through by his collar. He seemed reluctant to go any further.

'I don't think he likes this place,' said Harry.

'Don't blame him, either. It's spooky,' whispered Jack.

He kept behind Harry as they made their way forward. The tunnel seemed to go on and on. There was no sound but the drip, drip, of water.

'Hey! Come on, Raf,' called Harry.

They could see Raf hanging back near the doors. He came forward slowly, and they all started off again.

The tunnel hadn't been used since the beginning of the war. Odd bottles lay about, and empty cases and half-made barrels littered the way. The boys picked their way along carefully.

Suddenly, they realized that Raf was no longer with them.

Harry flashed his torch back along the tunnel. They could see Raf leaning against the wall. When Harry called, he stumbled towards them.

'What's the matter with him?' said
Jack, worriedly.

When Raf reached the boys, he sank
slowly to the ground.

'Poor dog. What it is?' they said,
bending down to him.

Raf sighed deeply and rolled over.

'He's drunk!' cried Harry.

Raf looked blearily at Harry and yawned a great yawn.

A blast of wine-laden breath hit the boys in the face. Then Raf sighed again, and fell into a deep sleep.

'That's done it,' said Harry. 'Now I'll have to carry him!'

He put his arms around Raf's chest, and stood up. At once, he staggered back with the weight of the sleeping dog. Raf was so long that his back legs scraped along the floor. His nose was rammed under Harry's chin, and his front legs stuck out.

Jack giggled. Harry slumped against the wall of the tunnel. 'We'll have to think of something else,' he gasped.

'I know, let's make a stretcher,' suggested Jack.

They took off their jackets and tied the sleeves together, making a kind of bed. Harry rolled Raf into it. They grabbed hold of their jackets and stood up. Their stretcher sagged a bit in the middle but it was OK.

'His legs are dangling over the edge!' laughed Jack.

'He doesn't care,' said Harry. 'Come on.'

They made their way forward again, but Raf was heavy and they had to rest a lot. Jack was a year younger than Harry and not so strong.

'We've been down here for hours,' he said. 'I bet we'll be in trouble when we get home.'

'I think we're in trouble right now,' said Harry, in a low voice. 'Can you see what I see?'

Jack groaned. 'Oh no, I don't believe it! Not again.'

The boys stood horrified.

In front of them, the tunnel had fallen in. There was no way forward!

'I'm very scared, Harry,' whispered Jack. His voice wobbled.

'I've got to think,' said Harry, trying not to show how frightened he was. 'I've got to think. Put Raf down for a minute. Switch off the torches to save the batteries.'

'Let's not stand here in the dark!' begged Jack, close to tears.

But, bravely, he did as his brother told him, and they both stood in the pitch-black tunnel listening to one another breathing.

They stood there for perhaps a minute, though to Jack it seemed like ten, when Harry suddenly yelled:

'Light – there's light.' He clutched Jack's arm. 'There's light. See it?'

Jack peered into the darkness.

He could just see a chink of light through the pile of rubble in front of them. They put their torches on again and grinned at each other. 'Let's go!'

They dragged Raf to a safe distance and attacked the mess that barred their way.

They scrabbled madly at the broken brickwork, pulling and tossing the lumps aside.

Soon, they had cleared a small hole, and through it they could just see moonlight.

'Yes!' cried Harry. 'Nearly there! Keep going, keep going!'

Both boys doubled their efforts, gasping, grunting and coughing, as their aching arms gradually cleared a hole big enough to squeeze through.

'OK. That's big enough,' said Harry. 'Phew!'

He wiped the sweat from his face, and looked at Raf. He was fast asleep. 'It'll be hours before he wakes up. You go first, Jack. I'll push him and you pull.'

Jack clambered into the hole and wriggled through. Harry saw Jack's pale face peering back at him from the other side.

'Harry!' hissed Jack. 'You won't like it out here.'

'What!' called Harry. 'Now what are you on about?'

He started to bundle Raf into the hole. It wasn't easy. Raf seemed to have so many legs, and Harry had never seen anything flop about so much.

Every now and then Raf snorted loudly, blowing dust into Harry's face. All the time, he could hear Jack muttering from the other side.

'Shut up, Jack! Grab hold of his collar and pull.'

Raf suddenly disappeared through the opening, and Harry followed just in time.

As he scrambled through, an avalanche of bricks slithered down behind him. There was no going back.

Harry choked and rubbed his eyes clear of dust. What he saw made his stomach lurch with terror.

'No,' he whispered. His voice shook. 'It's that bomb! It's the one we saw from the warehouse! It can't be true!'

But it was true. There was no mistake. The terrible shape loomed above them.

Its metal casing gleamed in the moonlight. They could almost reach out and touch it. They had come face to face with the bomb!

CHAPTER 4

Fear

'I said you wouldn't like it out here,' said Jack. 'I'm scared.'

'Shut up!' said Harry.

They stood, frozen with terror, staring at the bomb. This was the end.

At last, Harry pulled himself together. 'Jack,' he said in a low voice. 'Let go of Raf's collar. You're choking him.'

Jack let go. The dog slid to the ground with a happy sigh and slept on.

The moonlight made everything look as bright as day. The sides of the crater were sheer, and the soil was loose and sandy.

Jack reached up and tried to get a foothold, but the soil gave way under his shoe, and he fell back against Harry.

Both boys staggered together, almost on top of the bomb. Small stones rattled down the sides of the crater, pinging and bouncing off the metal. Harry and Jack clung to one another, numb with fear.

'Move back slowly,' whispered Harry.

They moved back – slowly – very slowly.

They reached the side of the crater and Jack's knees gave way. He slid to the ground and closed his eyes.

Harry sat down beside him and spoke softly. 'We must keep still. It might have a trembler.'

Jack opened his eyes. 'What's a trembler?'

'It's a thing that sets off the explosive. If there is a sudden noise or movement – Bang!'

Raf snored loudly. Harry clamped Raf's jaws together, and stroked his shaggy head.

'He's having a dream.'

'I wish I was,' said Jack. His voice shook. 'Harry, I've just thought. Will they blow up the bomb here?'

'Don't be daft,' said Harry. But his face was pale. They dragged Raf across their legs to keep them warm, untied their jackets and put them back on.

'What's going to happen to us, Harry? I wish we were back home with Mum.'

'They'll come and find us in the morning. They've got to. We've just got to wait.'

As the moonlight shone down, they waited as if made of stone. Hours went by and they stayed still – the two boys – the dog – and the bomb.

CHAPTER 5

Rescue

Dawn came slowly. A shaft of sunlight reached into the crater, making the metal glint and shine. The boys were numb and stiff, and hungry. They tried not to look at the huge shape that loomed over them.

Harry suddenly opened his eyes and clutched at Jack's arm.

'Listen!' he whispered.

Jack's eyes widened instantly, and both boys strained their ears.

They could hear a man talking softly. The voice seemed a long way off. Jack went to shout, but Harry clamped his hand over Jack's mouth.

'Don't shout,' he hissed. 'We'll be blown to pieces.'

The soft voice came nearer and nearer. Suddenly, an army captain appeared at the top of the crater. He was talking into a mouthpiece strapped round his neck. He stopped talking when he saw the boys, and blinked several times.

'What the … ' he said. 'Who are you?' he asked softly.

Harry found his voice. 'Jack and Harry Brown,' he croaked.

'Is that dog dead?' asked the captain.

'No, he's drunk,' said Harry.

The captain blinked again, and passed a tired hand over his face. A squawking voice came from a box on his shoulder.

The captain opened his eyes and spoke into the mouthpiece.

'Sergeant,' he said. Then he stopped and took a deep breath before he went on. 'There's two kids and a drunken dog down here.'

A single squawk came from the box.

The captain crouched down and stared closely at the bomb. 'Don't move and don't speak,' he said, 'or we'll all go up.' He began talking quietly to his sergeant.

Jack and Harry were too stiff to move. They clung on to Raf, and waited.

Another man appeared at the top of the crater.

'I thought so,' said the man. 'It's them all right.'

'It's Old Tin Hat!' whispered Jack. 'He'll kill us.'

Old Tin Hat was carrying a ladder.

He and the captain lowered it into the
loose earth next to the boys.

'Keep still,' the captain warned them.

As the captain held on at the top, Old Tin Hat started to come down the ladder very slowly, very gently – step by step.

At last he reached the bottom, and with one movement, he lifted Jack on to his back.

Harry watched as Jack was carried up. It seemed to take an age.

There was a sudden fall of earth, and Old Tin Hat froze halfway up. Harry gasped with terror but the ladder didn't move. Old Tin Hat started up again, and when he got to the top, hands reached out and Jack disappeared.

Old Tin Hat started down the ladder again – very slowly – one rung at a time. At last he got to the bottom.

Harry clung on to Raf. 'I'm not leaving him,' he whispered.

'Dog goes last, sonny,' said Old Tin Hat, softly.

'I'm not leaving him,' Harry whispered again, clutching Raf tighter than ever.

Old Tin Hat sighed. He crouched down beside Harry, and they stared at one another with the dog between them.

'OK,' Old Tin Hat said at last. 'Come on.'

He stood up and pulled Harry on to his back. Then he scooped up Raf and hunched him under one arm. This sudden movement woke Raf, who peered round, looking very surprised.

Old Tin Hat started to climb the ladder for the second time.

One rung, two rungs, three rungs, four rungs – he went very slowly, heaving himself from one rung to the next.

The weight of the boy and the dog made him gasp.

The climb up the ladder was a long one, and the rough uniform tickled Harry's nose, making him want to sneeze.

Raf just hung in the air looking rather silly.

At last they were at the top. The captain was bending over the ladder.

He grabbed Raf's collar and yanked him over the edge. Then came Harry and Old Tin Hat.

A faint cheer rose from a long way off, and Harry could see a group of people crowded behind a barrier. He could see Jack, with a blanket wrapped round him, and Mum, looking pale and worried. There was an ambulance and an army truck.

Old Tin Hat trod his way gently across the bomb site, followed by the captain, who was carrying Raf. When they reached the barrier, Harry's mum threw a blanket round his shoulders and gave him a big kiss.

'Mum! Am I glad to see you!' laughed Harry.

'Warden, you're a hero!' said someone.

'No, there goes the hero,' said Old Tin Hat, pointing to the captain, who was making his way back to defuse the bomb. Old Tin Hat pushed his hat back to wipe his forehead.

'We always thought your hair was grey!' cried Jack.

'Much more of you and it will be!' joked Old Tin Hat.

Raf jumped up at Harry's mum.

'Good boy, Raf,' she said. 'You can be our dog now.'

Raf wagged his squashed tail, and licked her face. 'Ugh!' she cried.

Later on when the bomb was defused, the captain came over and spoke to Harry and Jack. 'Your bomb is safe now. Want to have a look?'

'Yes, please,' said the boys. 'Come on, Raf.'

Harry and Jack followed the captain, and Raf scampered along beside them. They went over to the army truck. It had 'BOMB DISPOSAL' on the side.

The bomb was already loaded on to the truck, and the boys watched it as it was tied into place. It looked different now – like a stranded whale. The boys remembered the hours in the crater and they shivered.

The captain climbed into the truck. 'Cheerio!' he shouted.

The truck rumbled off down the street.

The bomb in the back wobbled a bit, in a helpless sort of way. They watched the grey shape getting smaller. Finally the truck rounded a corner, and the bomb was gone.

Harry and Jack and Raf turned away, and ran towards home.

About the author

I was a school teacher at
first, and then I became
a professional pianist.
I found writing was
fun and helped me to
relax, and I have had
a number of stories
published.

I now live in Norfolk, but my family
came from the East End of London,
which is the setting for *Air Raid!* As a
small child, I can remember what it was
like to be bombed, and I can tell you it
was very frightening. I'm glad that you
will live it only through my words.